# THE AHA MOMENTS

**Also by Vera Dragilyova**

IDEASTHESIA

CURVES IN CULTURE

THE BEST OF ALL WORLDS

LIFE AS ART

# THE AHA MOMENTS

*Little Thoughts for Your Eyes Only*

Vera Dragilyova

*Verarta Books*

# CONTENTS

# INTRODUCTION

This is a compilation of little thoughts, to inspire mental flight and experimentation.

Brain is a muscle that makes us live longer, if trained regularly.

Little brain candy is both a candy and an exercise, making thinking the most pleasant diet in the world.

Thinking can actually stretch your mind until you feel as big as the universe. And it is a good feeling to have, especially because we only have so much time to live.

Brain candy a day keeps the doctor away!

## WHAT HAPPENED BEFORE

Mr. Reed Wright was a good man of strong morals, and of old age. He had been collecting little thoughts here and there, all his life, as a proof to himself that he once existed. Now and then, he would glance at these pages and smile, as his whole life would rush in front of his eyes, word for word.

Once, his ten-year-old nephew Toochki snuck into his office, out of pure curiosity, and searched inside his wooden desk. Reaching out into the back corner of a dusty drawer, Toochki felt a sudden pinch. He drew out his hand, and saw a little red line crossing the tip of his index finger, blood coming out. A paper cut! Angered, Toochki reached in again, stretching his arm even further, finally grabbing onto a stack of papers, and pulled them out.

On the top page, there were strange lines, scribbled in dark purple ink, smeared in some places, as if someone had cried over them and wiped off their tears.

"Only a chicken foot could have a handwriting like that!"—thought Toochki. Holding the stack in his hands, his finger in pain, Toochki just stood there, listening to his heart beat, as if it were a clock. After all, these could be directions to a hidden treasure! But then, it could also be just an old journal, full of who knows what. It is as if his heart was drumming to read or not to read?—when he saw a huge hand reaching over his shoulder and covering the papers.

"Uncle!"—he screamed.

"Toochki, where did you get these?"

"They came to me on their own."

"You were looking for money in my desk, confess now!"

*I was only looking for a treasure.*

"I was only looking for a treasure."

"Well, you found it. It is in your hands."

"And how many ice creams can I buy for these?"

"You can't buy happiness, you know."

"Then, you can have these back,"—said Toochki, pouting, and handed the papers back to his uncle Reed.

"Oh, that is what I expected. You are sure?"

"Yes, I am, just let me go!"

"How sad it is to see your progeny to be so indifferent to who you were, once you die."

"What? Is that even English?"

"Never mind. I will just burn these."

"Whatever,"—Toochki shrugged his shoulders and lowered his eyes. Uncle Reed walked to the window and looked out into the sky.

"Oh, and, there is something I wanted to tell you. Toochki?"—started Mr. Wright, but Toochki had already gone.

Mr. Wright was always right about things, and this time he knew what to do. He mumbled to himself, as if singing a song: "Whoever can read these lines, can write themselves a new life story. Some money in the bank, some thoughts in the drawer, and I am good to go."

"Where are you going?"—asked Toochki.

"I thought, you left!"—Mr. Wright turned around.

"What's in those papers?"

"Ah, so you are not after the money, after all?"

"All I want is ice cream, uncle Reed, but also, where are you going?"

"From where no traveler returns, my son."

"Don't go, uncle Reed."

"Read these. It is for your eyes only: that is all the ice cream my money could buy."

"Not now, later,"—pouted Toochki.

"Then, here is some money. Go buy yourself an ice cream,"—Mr. Wright stretched out his hand with a few wrinkled dollars in it. Toochki sparkled a smiled, and, with his eyes still lowered, grabbed the money out of his uncle's hand. Mr. Wright patted

Toochki on the back, and followed him with a glance, as Toochki sprung out of the room.

Now, Mr. Wright settled in his chair, took a deep sigh, and, spreading the stack of papers on the table, started reading.

## POLITICS AND SOCIETY

The more innocent a soul, the more susceptible to corruption it is.

Law is an ever-changing attempt to serve justice that always stays the same.

Individualism in a society is like a leaf on a tree who says to the other leaves: "You all, I don't like what you are all doing, so I am out. I am leaving!"

Life is hard for those living like neo-nomads and historical orphans.

The world is cyclical: neo-savages, then neo-nomads, then neo-slave-masters.

Passion and ignorance are a lethal combination.

Unhappy people are dangerous to the society.

Not having a strategy is like sending out a train with no rails ahead.

Hard work purifies the soul.

Yesterday's innovation: reinventing the wheels in a new way. Today's innovation: new choices of reinvented wheels. Tomorrow's innovation: new ways of looking at choices of reinvented wheels.

Arguing for a total freedom of media would be like trying to eat everything, including garbage and sewage, to protect yourself from becoming too selective and missing some important vitamins.

Countries are recognized by their villains, and people—by their faults.

Unfiltered media use our instinctual focus on danger to popularize and legitimize things that are bad for us.

*Money knows no loyalty.*

One can wreak havoc on a group by changing the discussion from what results everyone wants and to how to get there.

Decide carefully, move quickly, and carry a magic wand.

Strategy: if we go anywhere, we will get nowhere.

Differences of political systems are only disagreements on the practical application of the same moral values.

In a fight without rules, the one who follows rules will lose.

Eventually, public workers become as good as the worst of the public that they serve—who are but a small minority—to the great amazement of the majority of the public, who wonder where such severity originated.

A democratic vote is least representative when opinions differ greatly.

A constant appeal to the unpredictability of the unknown reveals one's cunning intent.

Strategy is the long-term answer for the everyday *why* of the tactics.

War is about what I want, business—about what you want. War is a zero-sum game, business—a Prisoner's Dilemma.

A group is as successful as the current vision of its most dominant member, while the group's potential is the best vision of *any* member.

A high degree of public criticism only testifies to a high degree of public importance.

People misuse the internet just the same as they misuse religion

It only takes one single generation that discounts their history to destroy a long-standing civilization.

Public coverage of protests makes them socially approved and contagious, just like what it does for suicides.

Liberals are free radicals, and conservatives are free hoarders.

Law is pure entertainment, both for criminals and for lawyers. For both, the goal is to get around it and away with it.

Nationalism is like a body's overactive autoimmune reaction, socially manifested.

The momentum of politics is in ignorance of the masses.

A modern country is not a country, it is an organization.

*Revolution is not a solution.*

Fight your fear of the unknown and your habit of inaction.

The more passionately they criticize you, the more they envy you. If you were not that important, they would not even bother.

Low self-esteem is so destructive that it should be considered a sin.

To change the world for the better, avoid protests and revolutions. Instead, get educated and assume positions of power, from where you can directly wield your influence.

People gravitate and regress toward social and economic systems that reward them for their natural behaviors and require minimal change and effort.

A civilization of savages is a dangerous thing.

This generation is the state of degeneration. That is what they always say.

One cannot create a sustainable community based on a conscious effort of everyone—but only based on everyone's natural desire. Conscious effort requires a continuous input of energy, and a natural desire is the energy itself. That is why Communism failed and Capitalism is still alive.

Sometimes, we sacrifice what makes us happy, just to earn the right to choose another option, an option we never wanted. This is how much we are willing to pay for our freedom.

Communism is an impossibly extreme form of democracy.

An honest salesman should not be an oxymoron. Otherwise, it would be ethical to call a salesman moron.

As long as people do not know why they want what they want, they are easily manipulated.

Our personal differences are far greater than our racial or ethnic similarities.

Democracy is government publicly owned.

Communism is the most abstract religion in the history of humanity.

Politics is masses of people serving individual ambition.

Loving your neighbor and stupidity are incompatible.

Extreme wealth forces you into reverse prostitution: other people serve you by invading your intimate space, and you pay them for it.

*Sensitivity breeds cruelty.*

People misuse the internet just the same as they misuse religion.

In an honest fight, the victory is with the dishonest.

In a fight without rules, the one who follows rules will lose.

The real malnutrition crisis is the lack of oxytocin.

The real original sin is that we are born without equal abilities.

Idealism is the necessary good to counterbalance the necessary evil.

Fight your fear of the unknown and your habit of inaction.

Democracy is government publicly owned.

A modern country is not a country, it is an organization.

One cannot create a sustainable community based on a conscious effort of everyone—but only based on everyone's natural desire. Conscious effort requires a continuous input of energy, and a natural desire is the energy itself. That is why Communism failed and Capitalism is still alive.

Sometimes, we sacrifice what makes us happy, just to earn the right to choose another option, an option we never wanted. This is how much we are willing to pay for our freedom.

Communism is an impossibly extreme form of democracy.

As the world is changing right before my own eyes, I stand in awe and stupefaction, unable to move an inch.

When stakes are sufficiently high, any competition, if left unchecked, quickly changes from competing on quality to competing on destruction. A dead person cannot compete, just as an absentee cannot win in court.

Democracy creates an erroneous sense of equal vote, because ignorance and incompetence, bias and partiality, intellectual ability and indoctrination —are not a factor. Since there is no filter for social differentiation, democracy is still the best system we have got.

We commonly agree on the good to which we aspire, but how to get there is an eternal area of disagreement. Unite, then conquer with one stone.

Religion has little to do with God, when it stresses rules and rituals in lieu of spirituality and understanding.

*Ignorant power is lethal.*

We commonly agree on the good to which we aspire, but how to get there is an

Popularity is often a false positive. eternal area of disagreement.

A successful organization is a flock of leaders with a clear sense of direction and a common goal.

Lenin, Hitler, and Pol Pot all were rejected by the system in their youth, only to come back for revenge.

One way to know whether a society is healthy is by observing whether its women get along.

There is a reason surgery is not a democratic process. So, why do we vote for politicians, if we have no idea about how politics is done?

Revolution does not change the system, it destroys it.

Collectively, people constitute a new chemical element "Hu", and it is very similar in its structure and behavior to water.

In a society with total competition, total freedom of choice means total self-destruction.

The act of suing a lot should be called sewage. Ah, English language!

It is not stupidity in itself but acting on it that causes social harm.

A wounded enemy must be killed.

Societies that do not care for their women do not develop, those that do not care for their elders —degrade, and those that do not care for their children—perish.

The measure of one's political success should not be popularity, but by the aggregate happiness one's political activity has precipitated.

Some cultures are an acquired taste, and some acquire you as soon as you meet them.

Democracy is a form of monarchy, where media are the monarch.

It is all about the ideology of strategy and in the practicality of tactics.

Keep your thinking headquarters to your head —far from limbs, as you would a country's capital —from its borders.

I am not interested in people's money: I am interested in their ideas.

God knows no religion. Some people know religion but not God.

*Poverty breeds creativity.*

One of the greatest perils of democracy is reducing the human function to its lowest common denominator.

Divide and conquer is not always the best strategy. It is easier to walk on asphalt than on sand.

A knife made of steel is stronger than a plastic knife. Tightly organized systems are more powerful, but also are easier to control, and that is their paradox.

You ask why I don't vote? Because voting feels like gambling.

In every culture, there are docile wolves and ravenous rabbits.

Globalization is a social and cultural antibiotic. Cultural exchange is an organic fertilizer.

The influence of leaders is judged by the resistance they have overcome, and by the size and number of battles they have fought and won.

Vision is the why, mission is the what.

I have no time for being super-rich.

There is a humongous fungus among us.

The progress is in the process, the results are hidden, and the bottomline is not the bottom that it seems.

The bigger the country, the harder it is to manage, the more cruel are its measures, and the more psychopathic behavior it tolerates.

Diversity is about differences. Complexity is about how those differences interact.

Communal celebration confirms to the society that it exists.

President of a country is the ultimate customer service position.

Violence is highly contagious.

## MIND AND KNOWLEDGE

Wait! Let's savor the moment of not knowing.

My favorite sport is thinking.

Common sense is not that common.

Teaching is the art of midwifery of ideas.

If you cannot win in a game, question its rules.

Understanding means making ever-finer distinctions and ever-broader generalizations.

Heart-mind is a false dichotomy.

First language is like filling up an empty vessel. Learning the second language is expanding the vessel to fill it up.

Something we do not understand—we call either crazy or genius. If we presume ourselves smarter than it is—then, it is crazy. If we presume it to be smarter than us—then, it is genius. Yet, sometimes, something is simply misunderstood.

The breadth of one's experience contributes to the depth of one's understanding.

Do not reject zany ideas based on what you know, but give them a chance based on what you don't.

Zany ideas might be wrong, but the ideas they inspire might be right.

Pure chaos is as conceptually elusive as pure perfection.

Your most powerful thinking tool is your well-informed intuition.

*Time creates the illusion of space.*

The limit of the speed of light is reflected everywhere—it is in how fast a water drop will fall, in how fast the sound of thunder reaches your ears, and how fast we age. The speed of everything is tuned to a certain measure, and its range regresses to a single setting—the radio station of God.

There is nothing complicated in this world. All that seems complicated—is simply new.

We always either fear the unknown or idealize it, but we don't ever expect it to be ordinary.

Religion and science are both an offspring of philosophy, except religion uses pure intuition for its scientific method.

Research has been reduced to sifting through the historical details of who said what and the order in which it happened, a deadly minutia that is more gossip-like and sensationalist than truth-seeking. It encumbers the researcher's mind and obscures the fundamental principles and the gist of the matter.

Diligent but not intelligent.

Chaos Theory is the new theology.

I have a psychological allergy to entropy.

I have a psychological allergy to ignorant, opinionated people.

Any religion or philosophy develops a consciousness to a certain level, and then holds it back from developing any further. So, conceivably, a teaching can cause a degradation of mind.

I may be naive, but I am not stupid.

Complexity is cyclically simple, like fractals.

Our common sense depends on how much we have in common.

There is the social glitch that stifles discovery: a statement is always asked for more proof than the response that attacks it.

Ignorance is at the root of naive indifference that, unbeknownst to itself, condones all evil.

I enjoy milking my brain for insight.

Consciousness and subconsciousness are essentially a partitioned hard drive, where one part does all the work and the other one—all the thinking about it.

Everything is easy: it is just a matter of explaining it right.

Posing a question necessarily stipulates the rules for the answer.

*Ignorance is fear.*

Building an artificial brain is like creating a whole culture overnight—with its traditions, personal connections, history, and emotional baggage.

What do TV, car, and knife have in common? They all fully depend on their users to do good or harm.

There will always be something new that no one has thought of before. It is because, statistically, there are more thought combinations possible than there are particles in the universe.

Our new-and-improved work process: forget-the-past-and-reinvent-many-versions-of-wheels-then-debate-about-choice-to-reductio-ad-absurdum. Lots ado about, and everyone is right in their own way. The progress is in the process. And the results are obvious.

Modern science is an excellent tool for idea analysis, and an excellent tool against idea creation.

Any attempt to represent an idea necessarily distorts the idea itself.

Bell curve is really a belle curve.

That no one can see what you see does not make you wrong.

Think in five senses instead of sentences.

Study until you feel like throwing up or until you get really good at it, or whichever comes first.

I love questions, I eat them for dinner.

Saying that I don't know exculpates me from any logical fallacy.

Don't dump on me everything you know. Just give me a few simple and far-reaching ideas.

No, I am not crazy. It is just that your hardware is not ready for my software.

Learning to translate is learning a whole new language.

You always know when it is your first time, but never really know when it is your last.

So many words have turned clichés that we are running out of words to express ourselves in unique ways. Unique is one of them, cliché—another.

Neither Aristotle nor Einstein went to Harvard, and they didn't have a computer.

The first stop toward knowledge is knowing what you don't know.

*Emotion informs logic.*

Math is just another game with a lot of rules.

Raise your hand, those who thought it but did not say it.

When you find yourself having to dumb down what you have to say, so as to avoid being treated with aggression, then you know that you are decidedly smarter than the other person. And it's a very unpleasant feeling.

There are no a wrong answers, there are only answers that are almost right.

Selective ignorance is individualized bliss.

It is not that I know too much. I understand too much.

When my brain stops worrying, it starts thinking.

Knowledge is the most renewable food source in the world.

What we understand—we call science, what we don't—we call art.

Every lengthy word problem can be reduced to a concise mathematical statement.

There are people who give boring answers to boring questions—commonplace, the lost. There are those that give boring answers to interesting questions—those are the worst, the burden. There are those who answer interesting questions with interesting answers—they are the engine of progress. Yet, only the best of the best can answer boring questions with interesting answers—they are the engineers of the world.

What matters in group work is not agreement, but an equal level of mental agility.

Crabwork—a neologism, meaning engagement in busy work that involves a great deal of entropy, with an exorbitant number of requirements, unclear scope, and usually dubious outcomes.

I believe in God, but I am not religious enough to convert to any religion.

Logic is only instrumental to the emotional value of the outcome.

We cannot make a rational decision without weighing the emotional value of each possible outcome.

Stereotyping is overused, but only because it is useful.

The challenge of searching for the truth is in asking the right questions. The answers leading to the truth will follow.

*I can't remember everything I know.*

The Universe is a giant complex adaptive system, just like the brain.

My thoughts are like a body of water that assumes whatever shape it enters.

I did not say it: I only thought it. In fact, I only thought of thinking it.

When intelligence and ignorance meet, intelligence blames itself and ignorance blames intelligence.

That same dogma that once elevated you, will one day stifle your potential.

To think just a little is enough to destroy things, but not enough to create.

One should always think well, or not at all. To think just a little is dangerous.

Some arguments cannot be won with propositions that appeal to logic, but rather with throwing an experience on the opponent, which will, as a result, appeal to their intuition.

Theories is what I eat for breakfast.

Human mathematics is object-based, but mathematics of nature is based on relationships. Humans count objects and derive numbers, whereas nature perceives synthesis and derives ratios.

Our universe is one giant fractal whose algorithm constantly evolves.

The brain sees the body as a protective shell.

Meditate or vegetate?

Fat and sugar have a lot in common: $c_{60}h_{92}o_6$ and $c_6h_{12}o_6$.

It is not all in your mind! There is a boisterous reality outside, whether you want it, doubt it, deny it, or not.

Tragedy of the Commons is what happens when the Prisoner's Dilemma fails.

What is missing in this puzzle is the puzzle itself.

We are what we think, we are what we do, and we become that on which we choose to focus.

Brain is the ultimate IoT machine.

A ) smiley is an abbreviation of an emoticon.

Reality is not digital— it is analog. Even the real numbers are not real—they are digital.

*I am a bit agnostic.*

It's nothing personal: it's all science.

Mathematics is purely descriptive, to the point of tautology.

Every rule has an exception, including this very rule.

Truth can only be descriptive, but not imperative.

The degree of awareness is not only an indication of intelligence, but also of being alive. Extreme awareness might mean genius, but extreme lack of awareness is death. This way, life and intelligence are equivalent.

Make your concept waterproof and bulletproof.

Much of education is merely reconfirming what one already knows.

Our thinking cannot avoid being recursive, and that is our greatest limitation.

This is a really good question that may not have a good answer.

Having a front and a back, top and a bottom, reminds us of time—this is how plants, animals, and even comets move through space, as the time passes.

If you want to hear mathematics, listen to music.

I do not follow anyone except my better judgment and my heart.

Mathematics is the best brain muscle builder, only seconded by music.

Don't be a walking encyclopedia: be a learning machine.

I can't remember what I forgot. Ha! That's an almost perfect unknown unknown.

The worst thing about ignorance is not lack of knowledge, but the close-mindedness and aggression against new information that accompany it.

I am only a pattern in energy, but I promise—it's a fun one!

What are you doing? Swimming in my qualia.

Let's not offer qualitative solutions to quantitative problems and vice versa. Or maybe, they are the only solutions that there are?

There are three types of reviews: blind support, friendly critique, and hostile nonsense.

Knowledge is an extreme degree of faith.

*A circle is an eternal curve.*

Consciousness is a hallucination as much as hologram is a photo.

Any kind of insurance is reverse gambling. You are not gambling to win, you are gambling not to lose.

Those who know nothing fear nothing. Those who know everything—as well.

Ignorance is how good intentions result in evil actions.

If we want to see how our reality really works, we need to look at music under a microscope.

Mainland is still an island. Just a really big one.

The deeper I go into math, the more I realize that it is a religion.

Our universe is in the state of a very slow explosion, so slow that we feel that it stands still.

Innocence is a type of ignorance.

Social processes impeccably mirror the physical processes in our reality.

Learning a language is exactly like learning to ride a bicycle or to play piano.

I forgot what I didn't know, and now I can't even remember what I forgot.

If you drill a hole into the earth, and reach the people directly on the other side of the planet, you will find that they are standing upside-down.

What is the point of arguing, if you can never be sure of anything, anyway? Being sure is a continuum, and moving in the direction of certainty is all that matters.

Time is the reason for space.

# ARTS AND TECHNOLOGY

Creativity is the discovery of the unknown unknowns.

We are all more creative than we know it. It is just that our brain hides it from us so that we wouldn't go insane.

My stories are like the daily horoscope: if you look hard enough, you will find yourself in them.

I want to be an artist, just so I could have an artistic license to say what I want with no fear, have it considered merely art, and therefore beyond any censure or criticism, or any material consideration. Being trivial is an unexpected freedom and an unimaginable power. Fiat art, and fiat lux.

My limitations are my inspirations.

Having lived without feeling music is like not having lived at all.

Good design is like a Shakespearian play: with many layers that appeal to many types of audience.

As long as there is some uncertainty, there is always space for magic.

Limitations are the bounce walls for ideas, where, when ideas bounce, they explode into millions of alternatives.

Behind the scenes, politicians are really designers, and designers are really politicians.

Writing is like eating, but in the opposite direction.

In design, use your heart as a guide, your brain —as a tool, and your common sense—as a method.

MLT ratio: meaning per line of text.

The structure of a story is the same as the structure of water: it is impossible to grab, but takes the shape of the vessel that contains it.

One's thread is someone else's carpet.

So much of modern writing is dumping, so that modern reading has become dumpster-diving.

A film does not end until its last spectator dies.

I am for technology for the sake of people, not technology for the sake of technology.

In design, your best method is your common sense.

Modern art: he who looks will find.

Depression stifles creativity.

*Stress kills creativity.*

Modern art: he who looks will find.

All creativity needs a craving audience, even if imaginary.

I binge-write, I binge-love, and I binge-live.

When I wake up, I don't want to go to work—I want to start working.

To the audience: I feel that there is a little of me in each one of you, and that every one of you is in me. No idea how we all fit in there.

During procrastination, I have written more stories and seen more films in my head than there are words in all of my actual writing.

What suppresses sensitivity—kills creativity.

Art can be quantified and reduced to nothing, when ratings is all you have to count.

Creativity and sensitivity are highly correlated.

I love technology only when it provides maximum benefit at minimum effort.

In a story, all is well that ends well, and if it's not well—it ain't over!

A story starts with a character, but a character cannot start with a story, just like a person casts a shadow, but not the reverse.

Every story follows a trajectory of a heartbeat.

Writing fiction is being God within your imaginary world.

A movie is the bespoke fire of which the trailer smoke speaks.

A work of an artist is a continuous conversation about the meaning of life.

The image is not in the particles, but in the relationships between them.

Brining up what is intuitive to the surface can cause creative block. Some things are better left unexplained.

Story is not something we create, but it is something we discover, and then chose the pieces we tell.

Beauty is the algorithm of my world.

A story is a series of call and response, of action and reaction, like songs I have heard in Africa.

Instead of saying it, write it out loud.

Writing is bitter-sweet, more sweet than bitter.

Awe at the unknown is what sparks imagination

*There are a million of unborn stories...*

If you find yourself in a writer's block, it just means that you are trying too hard, you are too focused and too serious. Play a game and care less, and the block will vanish.

I never drink alcohol: it is all brewed locally. (Pointing to my head).

When on stage, please do not doodle—perform.

I don't know why, but writing 3000 words feels exactly like driving 300 miles. Exactly! That's 10 words per mile.

Fashion is driven by neophilia, xenophilia, and nostophobia. Sometimes—by nostalgia, when it runs out of rebellious ideas.

Every event and object in the universe has a structure of a story.

Transformation from color to black-and-white is a perfect example of abstraction.

Graffiti are city's tattoos.

A story writes itself instantaneously in my mind, and I might even believe it!

To allow media be controlled by ratings is like letting school subjects to be designed by the first graders.

When you listen to my stories, I re-live them through you.

There is no story without a problem.

Prototype is a tangible hypothesis.

The fear of the unknown is the antithesis of imagination, while imagination is what humans have in common with God.

I have no guts nor the calling.

There are three qualities to make art a work of genius: truth, vulnerability, and goodness. Plus, of course—unpredictability.

A writer is exactly like a sperm donor. The writing takes on a life of its own.

I am thirsty for art, but in my environment, one can exist only as a camel.

The best cure against writer's block is child's play.

# LOVE AND FRIENDSHIP

A crime against true love is a crime against the universe.

Your capacity for happiness equals your capacity for love.

Home is not a place, home is a person.

There are billions of people in this world, but we only need one family, one friend, and one love to be happy.

Every sea on earth is an ocean of love.

To love parents and children is an instinct, but to love a stranger as part of your family is something altogether miraculous. The most amazing love is that between two true lovers.

Under a microscope, documentaries are all fiction.

Amateurs do what they do for passion. Professionals do it for money, and if they do it for passion, then they are amateurs who get paid.

The distance does not discourage. It inspires.

Some people keep you in prison of their absence.

Best design is as transparent, gentle, and powerful as water.

I don't like to control people, I like people to control themselves.

If you want to be happy, you have to develop the capacity for happiness, and if you want to be in love, you have to develop a capacity to love.

*Sensitive does not mean weak.*

My internal meltdown is about to be followed by an external explosion.

Everything has some good and some bad for which we can love it. Everything has some good and some bad for which we can hate it. It is not about good or bad: it is about love or hate.

If you control someone you love, there will be nothing left in them to love you back.

The biggest killer of relationships: EGOISM.

With some people, you ask for a Socratic ear, and they offer you a Hegelian dialectic.

I don't know you well, but I know you well enough.

Girls are flowers, boys are leaves.

I am always searching for great thought companions.

Our difference in age will never change.

How deep are the crevices of un-love! How bitter is the taste of words that love, with the glance that doesn't. Even more bitter are the hidden tears for the one who loves you only with a glance.

If you get mad at me, I will get mad at you for getting mad.

Sometimes the impression is not bitter-sweet, but bitter-neutral, or worse— bitter-mysterious.

The less you give the less you expect and the less you get hurt. It really works. Yet, if everyone followed this formula, what a lonely world that would be!

I have spent so much time fighting my loneliness that I have become attached to it.

I don't want somebody to love me because of my kindness. I want somebody to love me despite my terrible nature.

It is everyone's sacred right to be loved with true love. And it is everyone's sacred responsibility to love someone with true love, at least once.

Sometimes what looks like strength is not strength at all, but a symptom of insensitivity and indifference.

The sun is always there. It is there even during the night—just on the other side of the planet!

I am worth 2 cents in my 10-cent world. Your world is—a billion dollars.

Give a chance to the chance.

It takes two to tango, and it takes three to make a love triangle. Some things are not meant to be done alone.

It's like to cry with your eyes closed.

Love is the greatest anesthetic known to humanity.

There is such great pain inside me that I no longer feel it. I just know that it's there.

We often make a decision based on a fleeting feeling that seems to last an eternity, completely unaware that it is our momentary decision that will last a lifetime.

Jealousy is the slowest form of suicide.

You cheated on me with your wife.

I took a deep breath into my soul.

Standing at the edge of the cliff.    A down blanket of euphoria, covering up an instance of inconceivable shame, when the weary are silenced in awe! It feels too beautiful to be sinful, and too sweet to last but a moment.    And so, all the more blissful.

I am at the edge of human capacity to feel.

It is not about you or me, it is about something bigger than both of us.

I didn't change my mood—I changed my mind.

The most erotic object in the world is a beautiful idea.

No, I haven't forgotten and I haven't forgiven. I simply don't talk about it.

Emotionally and mentally constipated.

Every relationship must have a honeymoon period, to set the standards for the future.

Sometimes talking to someone is like leaving a message on an answering machine.

Being in love is when there is not enough of you to feel all the love there is, and this person takes up your full capacity of senses and perception.

One's sense of humor is a litmus test for one's personality.

Pity is a form of violence against the object of the pity.

Bad relationships are like terrorists: they scare us into closing up to other people. It's probably not a good idea to give them what they want.

One who loves to love can never fall in love.

*I love you as if I will live forever.*

To wait is to count very slowly the heartbeats and the smiles than never come. It is longer than forever.

There are weddings for which you get ready with your heart and soul, and which feel like infinite divides between the old and the new life, and there are others: the moment of signing the papers is just like flushing the toilet.

Catch me if you can! But if you catch me, you better take care of me.

A man who enjoys women cannot love a woman. A woman who enjoys men cannot love a man. Love hurts.

Instead of saying that you disagree, just say what you have to say.

Just like one cannot see the puzzle without putting all the pieces together, just like glass shatters cannot make a cup to carry water, just like the fire will not start without focusing all light rays through a magnifying glass at one single point— so spending one's heart on little loves will not make for one true love or true happiness.

Why do you live far from your family?   I am incubating my marriage.

Sometimes I forget people, and only remember a memory of them.   An empty carcass, an aftertaste, a vestigial footprint on a road I never walked.

Life without love is like sea without salt.

Remember how they used to hunt bear in the forests of the Far East? You attach a knife to your heart and you hug the bear just right.

All four seasons of emotions in one day today!

You wanna bite?  Let me swallow you and then you can eat me from the inside.

Two twin beds is the sum of the parts. King bed is the greater whole. Amazing!

You feel safe with someone when they worry about you more than you worry about yourself.

You really should stop smoking and drinking. Drink and smoke me instead.

If you change yourself, you will also change to whom you get attracted.

Don't part with your loved ones, and when you leave for a moment, think of it as a lifetime.  A poet said it once.   This phrase sounds all the more painful when you realize that you are leaving someone you don't love, and the one you truly love —you have not found.

Some people are like the Moon: only one side that is always facing us, and they don't keep us warm. Some people are like the Sun: they keep us warm with every side they have.

## LIFE

A pearl is still a pearl, even if placed in mud and called a cherry pit.

The purpose of life is not in what but in how.

Some people are walking festivals, and some others—are lurking party-poopers.

I love life to death.

The more you live, the more life there is in you.

I want to jump out of myself and run away, and never-ever come back!

Yesterday I tried a little piece of beef—it was the best piece of chocolate I ever ate!

I am innocent, but I am not naive.

The two most scalable events in one's existence are birth and death. Birth is scalable until death, and death is scalable for infinity.

I keep redesigning myself all the time, so that not a molecule of mine would get lost in entropy!

Design yourself by yourself.

Once curious, always a traveler.

Does not look the part but does the job!

A secret to longevity is in eating when you are hungry, drinking when you are thirsty, and sleeping when you are sleepy.

I have a psychological allergy to mediocrity.

My new hobby is my job.

What is the solution between pessimism and optimism? It's pragmatism.

Want to get reincarnated in this lifetime? Just travel!

Off the grid, out of the system, away from the civilization!

If you could suddenly hear all the sounds of the world at the same time… Just imagine.

Earth is the only place where Heaven and Hell intersect.

One cannot travel twice to the same place, just like one cannot step twice into the same river. Or see the same sunset twice. Just like one cannot ever fit again into one's baby clothes. The place changes, and so do we. When traveling—carpe sensum, and choose wisely what you catch.

Magic exists.  Look for it.

After all, it is good that we are not immortals. This way, we never have to face the end of the world.

You cannot make me work at an office, just like you cannot staple water.

Money is not a necessary evil:  it is a necessary basic.

The moment you stop learning at work, you become disposable.

At work, people prefer machines when overwhelmed, and humans—when bored.

If nothing stays the same, there is always a chance for it to become better.

Driving a car is being a cyborg.

I have never mentally immigrated to where I live now. My mind is stuck in a place and time that exists no longer.

I live—therefore I feel. I feel—therefore I live.

Existentially anxious and opportunity cost aware.

Life is a huge prison, where everyone is on a death row.

Everything is instrumental to happiness.

I hate waste, unless it is emotionally motivated.

Carpe sensum! Seize the thought, and seize the feeling, as you would seize the day.

Opportunity cost is the hidden reason for not being.

What does not kill you, makes you stronger. Except sometimes it just makes you weaker, without killing you.

We forget the past as easily as our breath when we try to focus on it.

I don't believe in religion: I believe in God.

I live on planet number 30. That is my apartment number.

Cancer is a mushroom.

I don't want to be the greatest of all—I just want to be the greatest I can be.

The only pet I have now is my computer.

Time is a prison no one escapes.

*Life is an art form.*

Life is a prison, but our prison cells are so big, we have never seen the walls.

Don't try too hard to relax: it's counterproductive.

Some people float through empty moments that form into years of nothingness, and then they call it life.

You will find wonders, only if you wonder. And wander around.

I am always in search for a reason to be happy.

I am not hibernating: I am incubating.

I am old money, without the money.

Time flies, and I am still walking.

Feeling happy is sacred.

I am homesick for a place and time that exist no longer.

Those who feel hatred become a part of what they hate.

Being exposed to relative ignorance is as disgusting as being with a drunk person, without drinking yourself.

Death feels exactly like something you completely forgot. Better yet—like something you never knew.

Our whole life, we are slowly dying.

Dedicating one's life to making money is like hatching a really large egg with thick hard shell, only empty on the inside.

Savor everything you do.

The best thing about Christmas is not the gifts: it's the lights.

Life's changes are infinitely far in thought, and only one step away in action.

Do you know why time exists? It's because if you get everything, and all at once, you will explode.

Living is like swimming in fresh water: you can never just float.

Tomorrow is now.

There are no words in any human language to describe some human acts.

A successful person solves problems, while a loser—finds them.

First work smart, then hard.

*Faith is an extreme degree of hope.*

The greatest sign of God in us is our free will. Our ability to choose and act is the ultimate power of creation. We are all God, here and now.

Experiences vs. experiences of things.

I was already a 1000 years old when I was 5. 30 years later, it doesn't feel much different.

Time is a liquid that dilutes life.

Laughter is a reaction to stress.

Life is entropy shaped by an internal call and external response.

Depression is nothing but learned helplessness in the pursuit of pleasure.

Stuck in transition.

Today is a new day, and the first day of the rest of forever!

I have always had complicated dreams.

For an egoist, equality is having others serves them.

There are trees and flowers on this planet that have never seen a human. They don't even know that humans exist.

Student: May I go to the restroom?
Teacher: Yes, sure. That will be a $5 transaction fee, plus tax, plus tip, plus service charge and compound interest per minute you are gone. Can't pay now? Then it's a zero down, and you can pay in installments. If you fail to pay on time, you will be subject to non-graduation and late fees. Got it?

How can you blame devil for being evil?

That which makes you grow now—will stifle your growth one day.

Living feels like being squeezed flat between two perfectly flat slabs of granite, into a thin patina of life that slowly merges its molecules with stone, until it can no longer speak.

Just like an itch is the tiniest degree of pain, sadness is the tiniest degree of aggression.

A sure sign of growing up is acquiring a sense of disgust.

Living feels like carrying the whole ocean on my shoulders, my hands part flash part water, my hair — seaweeds, my eyes— the oyster shells, and my tears— the pearls. And the ocean is watching.

I am a mosquito serial killer.

*There are many ways of being.*

If the magic does not come to you, you have to search it out. If you don't find it—then you have to create it yourself. That's the secret of happiness.

Individual differences are far greater than cultural similarities, and cultural differences are far less significant than individual similarities.

This is how evil creeps into our lives: through innocence and ignorance.

Getting tired is just like compound interest: its gets increasingly worse as it progresses.

Sometimes you have to be stronger than yourself, in order to survive.

Those who love you will both criticize and applaud you. Beware of those who say nothing.

Be the best you can, and then stop wanting more —lest you become dangerous to others.

You are what you design yourself to be.

As long as you dream, you stay alive.

You certainly can't be liked by everyone. Yet, it is almost impossible that no one likes you.

We do not choose whom we are born, but other people choose us based on it.

Life right now is like life on the inside of a glass ornament, on a branch of a Christmas tree: you can see the magic on the outside but you cannot touch it.

This job was emotionally over-stimulating and intellectually under-stimulating, so I left.

Nature and the human mind are extreme opposites, in an eternal tug of war to establish order their way. Humans always lose.

Why worry? We will all die someday.

Listening is a selfish skill: it means taking from the world and not giving anything back.

Not listening is a useful skill, when what you will hear will harm you.

Every birthday, we don't get older—we add another year to our collection of life.

Nature knows no Friday, no rush hour, no last day of vacation.  It has its own clock and calendar, and even then—it does not follow them.

Skin has two sides and two surfaces—the outside and the inside, and we have to take care of both.

Take a picture with your eyes!  I took a picture with my heart.

Envy is essentially self-hatred.

*Each pearl was once an oyster's pit.*

I love New York, but not everything that feels good is good for you.

Slash and burn method sometimes is the best one to follow, in order to grow something.

Envy is essentially self-hatred.

You don't know who you really are until you find your happiness.

My life is a canvas I never paint. I see it grow 4D.

I love babies not because they are babies, but because they are people.

Sometimes you just need the ingredients—can't make a cake out of plastic!

As I get older, I don't change—I only add layers.

We love to hate.

They think I don't speak their language because, when they insult me, I smile.

There are no bad endings. If it ends bad, it ain't over!

Some use any holiday as an excuse to celebrate, and others—as a new reason for complaining.

Energy in a person can be channeled into change, defense, or growth.

Sometimes depression is simply a natural reaction to depressing circumstances.

Yes, the times have changed. It used to be dangerous to be around wild animals, and now—around wild people.

Society of one.

Children are not there to be abused, and they are not there to be obsessed about. They are there to be loved and understood, just like people of any age.

A 9-5 job is like religion: if you are lazy, it pulls you up, and if you are very active, it feels like prison.

Death is the ultimate bliss of ignorance.

I am not lazy, I am only against being waterboarded for a living.

Overworked! It's the case of when your own muscles break your own bones.

Our lives are like sand sculptures. You never know when the wave will come.

I don't eat food per pound, I measure food in units of pleasure.

*I prefer the best of all worlds.*

You have to control yourself, so you can control others.

You know why our tears are salty? They are a reminder that we all came from the sea, and it is still in all of us.

You can't lie about the future. That is why truth always wins—because it has happened already.

A pendulum is a sign of life.

So, what do you think about so and so? I don't think about her at all, but now that you ask, I should think about her. Let's see...

—Ma'am, you should get the family size. —If I get family size, I will become the size of a family!

Life is like a YouTube video with a lot of commercial pauses.

*Which drop am I in this ocean?*

Sometimes, the present moment feels like an eternity, and the eternity, ironically, feels like nothing.

Sometimes motivation and action do not align.

If you envy me, it means you like me. If you like me, it means that you are like me. If you are like me—why do you envy me?

Don't try to impress others: try to impress yourself.

She just lost it from all the worry. The question is where!

Asking me to become normal is like asking me to turn into a goat: I can't and I won't.

Listening to gossip is like sleeping with a prostitute: curious before, and disgusting after.

That's it! If by the end of this year, there is no butterfly emerging from me, I will stay a cutter pillar all my life.

Life is a dynamic evolving system that keeps some energy from escaping it into entropy. When the last of its energy escapes, the system dies.

A little water helps the fire, but too much of it— kills it.

I need a break. My brain is marinated, freeze-dried, deep-fried, chopped, tossed, and arranged on a platter in the form of a sushi roll, in a window of a restaurant in Tokyo. I am really out to lunch!

Technology in high doses becomes an emotional antibiotic.

I have a Russian soul, and an American spirit.

Old age is not an excuse for bad character.

Job-interviewing is exactly like speed-dating.

Travel sharpens all our five senses, and develops a sixth one.

Teacher is like a single parent—has to be a mother and a father at the same time.

When you travel, you interview a place as you would a person.

Give me the money, I will find the time. Give me the time, and money will not matter.

A picture is worth a thousand words, but an experience you cannot even buy with pictures.

When I wake up in the morning and look at my hair, I know that I am related to Einstein.

*Pleasure always wins over fear.*

We have an infinity of options in life, in a sense that the number of options is infinitely decreasing.

Being abused does not match any legal job description.

Ignorance and old age are a grotesque combination.

You are what you eat. And you eat what you cook. And you cook what you choose and buy at the market. So, you are essentially what you choose at the market. How funny!

When you travel, you are never alone—because nothing in the world is silent.

Throw it all together and let it cook itself.

Never do what you love for a living. Do it for the love of living.

And you, too, will grow old someday.

## WHAT HAPPENED AFTER

Mr. Wright looked out the window: the sun was setting over the horizon, its last rays reaching all the way to his face, making rainbow curls through his eyelashes. Their eyes met for a good long moment. Mr. Wright pulled out a metal trash can from underneath the table and stroke a match.

*Their eyes met.*

There was so much sun in this little flame, so much love for the past that was forever stacked in the drawers of time. Those little thoughts he gathered—no one, no one in the world laid their eyes on them. Except the flame devouring them right now, growing so much in power, it could have turned into a second sun.

Toochki leaped into his uncle's study, a heap of ice cream in his hand:

"Uncle Reed! Where are you? Look what I have got!" Toochki looked all around the room, under the table, and even in the drawer—but his uncle wasn't there.

"Oh, I know where to find you!"—yelled out Toochki.

Mr. Wright disappeared that night. The only thing he left behind was a pile of ashes and a note glued to the window, where the sun used to set every night. The note said: "For Your Eyes Only."

www.ingramcontent.com/pod-product-compliance
Lightning Source LLC
LaVergne TN
LVHW052032080426
835513LV00018B/2290